Atoms and MOLECULES MEET

Rebecca Woodbury, Ph.D., M.Ed.

Gravitas Publications Inc.

Atoms and
MOLECULES MEET

Illustrations: Janet Moneymaker
Design/Editing: Marjie Bassler, Rebecca Woodbury, Ph.D., M.Ed.

Atoms and Molecules Meet (hardcover)
ISBN 978-1-953542-58-8

Published by Gravitas Publications Inc.
Imprint: Real Science-4-Kids
www.gravitaspublications.com
www.realscience4kids.com

RS4K

Image credits: Cover & Title page: alexeevich, Adobe Stock. Above: Nikolai Titov, Adobe Stock. p. 3: Monkey Business, Adobe Stock. p.11: Aleksey, Adobe Stock. p. 13, Alexandre, Adobe Stock. p. 15, Ajamal, Adobe Stock. p. 17, Natalieime, iStock. p. 19. simonidad, Adobe Stock. p. 21 fizkes ,Adobe Stock

When you and your friends meet,
kids in the group might break apart
into smaller groups or switch partners
or rearrange into new groups.

Let's go over here!

Mice have friends too!

The same thing happens when
atoms and molecules meet.

Molecules can break apart, switch
partners, or rearrange their atoms
to make new molecules.

Atoms and molecules
are making new
friends!

Water molecule

Hydrogen

Sodium chloride
(table salt molecule)

Nitrogen

Review

- **Atoms** are tiny building blocks that can link together.

- **Atoms** make everything we see, touch, taste, and smell.

- We can draw **atoms** with arms and hands to represent **linking electrons**.

- **Atoms** link together to make **molecules** using their **linking electrons**.

Salt molecule

Oxygen

Carbon

Sodium   Chlorine

When atoms and molecules meet and rearrange, it is called a **chemical reaction**.

Pleased to meet you!

Hi!

Sodium   Chlorine

Hydrogen   Oxygen   Hydrogen

You can see **chemical reactions** when they happen.

- You might see **bubbles**.

- You might see **fire**.

- You might see a **color change**.

- You might see small **particles**.

- You might see **smoke** or **fumes**.

You can see a chemical reaction when sodium metal is added to water.

The water breaks apart and rearranges to make **hydrogen gas** that burns as fire.

Sodium metal

Water

Sodium hydroxide

Hydrogen gas

Chemical reaction between sodium metal and water

You can see a **chemical reaction** when water breaks apart to make **hydrogen gas** and **oxygen gas** using **electrical energy**.

Bubbles of hydrogen and bubbles of oxygen fill the test tubes.

Oxygen gas

Water

Hydrogen gas

Oxygen gas bubbles

Hydrogen gas bubbles

Water can break apart to make hydrogen and oxygen gas.

You can see a chemical reaction when molecules made of lead, nitrogen, oxygen, iodine, and potassium rearrange in a chemical reaction to make yellow particles called **lead iodide**.

Iodine　　Lead　　Iodine

**Lead iodide
molecule**

Pretty!

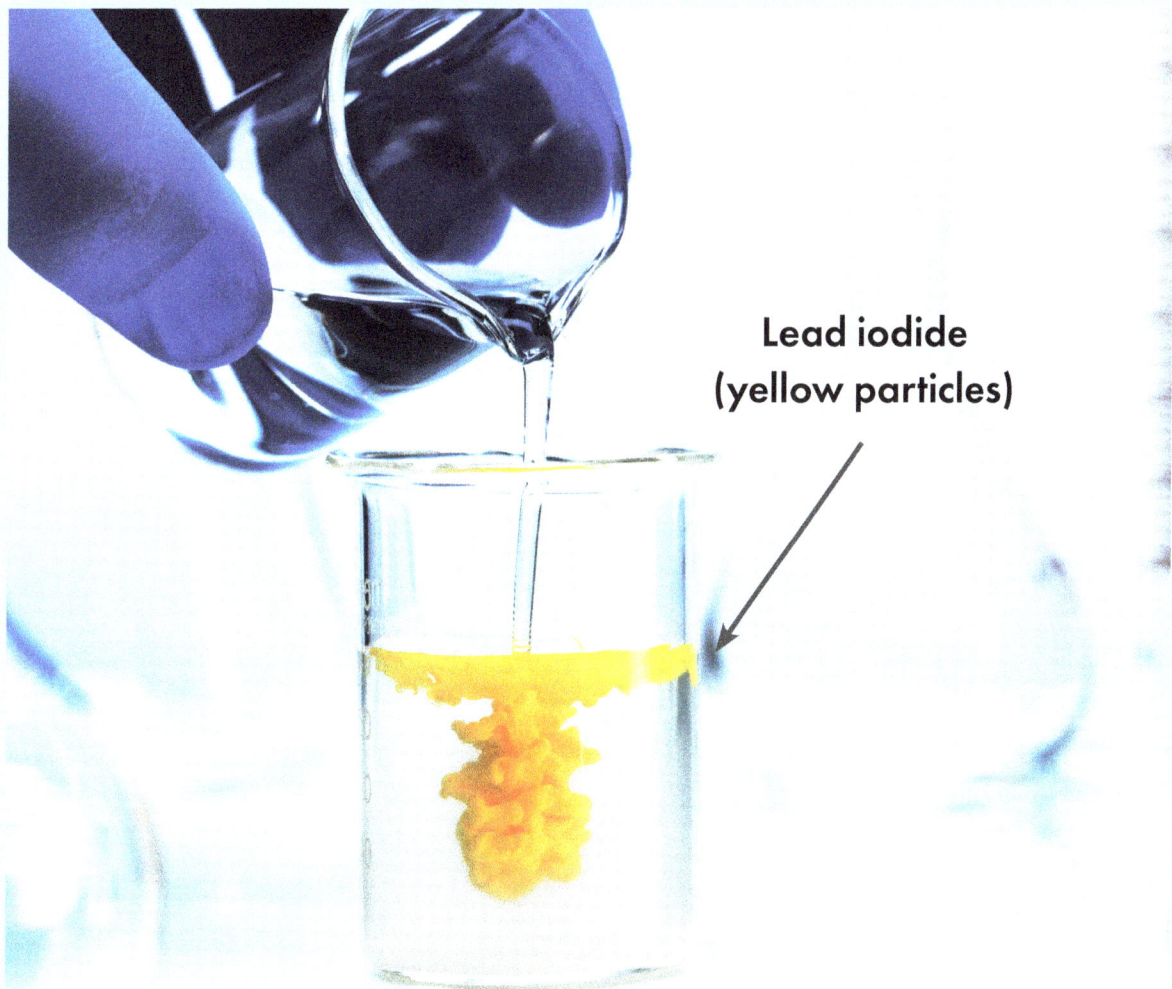

Lead iodide
(yellow particles)

Lead and iodine combine to make yellow lead iodide particles.

You can see chemical reactions when you make bread.

Yeast uses sugar to make **carbon dioxide**. The carbon dioxide bubbles make the bread rise.

Oxygen   Carbon   Oxygen

Carbon dioxide molecule

I like cheese.

I like bread.

Yeast uses sugar to make carbon dioxide bubbles.

Chemical reactions also happen in your body.

When you eat food, your body breaks it down to use for energy, to make bones, and to build muscle.

Chemical reactions happen everywhere!

How To Say Science Words

atom   (AA-tum)

carbon   (CAR-buhn)

chemical reaction
   (KEH-muh-kuhl ree-ACK-shun)

chlorine   (KLAW-reen)

electron   (i-LEK-trahn)

hydrogen   (HYE-druh-juhn)

molecule   (MAH-lih-kyool)

nitrogen   (NYE-truh-jun)

oxygen   (OCK-sih-jun)

particle   (PAHR-ti-kul)

phosphorus   (FAS-fuh-rus)

sodium   (SOH-dee-um)